ART and INVENTION

Inventions in Architecture

From Stone Walls to Solar Panels

Pamela D. Toler

Cavendish Square
New York

Published in 2017 by Cavendish Square Publishing, LLC
243 5th Avenue, Suite 136, New York, NY 10016

First Edition

Website: cavendishsq.com

CPSIA Compliance Information: Batch #CW17CSQ

All websites were available and accurate when this book was sent to press.

Library of Congress Cataloging-in-Publication Data

Names: Toler, Pamela D., author.
Title: Inventions in architecture : from stone walls to solar panels / Pamela D. Toler.
Description: New York : Cavendish Square Publishing, 2017. |
Series: Art and invention | Includes bibliographical references and index.
Identifiers: LCCN 2016033908 (print) | LCCN 2016034214 (ebook) |
ISBN 9781502623072 (library bound) | ISBN 9781502623089 (E-book)
Subjects: LCSH: Architecture and technology. |
Building--Technological innovations. | Building materials.
Classification: LCC NA2543.T43 T65 2017 (print) | LCC NA2543.T43 (ebook) |
DDC 720/.47--dc23
LC record available at https://lccn.loc.gov/2016033908

Editorial Director: David McNamara
Editor: Caitlyn Miller
Copy Editor: Nathan Heidelberger
Associate Art Director: Amy Greenan
Designer: Joseph Macri
Production Coordinator: Karol Szymczuk
Photo Research: J8 Media

The photographs in this book are used by permission and through the courtesy of: Cover Iain Masterton/Getty Images; pp. 6-7 David Wall Photo/Lonely Planet Images/Getty Images; pp. 12-13 CM Dixon/Print Collector/Hulton Archive/Getty Images; pp. 16-17 Geothea/Shutterstock.com; pp. 22-23 rasoulali/Shutterstock.com; pp. 24-25 Radomir Vrbovsky/File: Ishtar gate in Pergamon Museum in Berlin. jpg/Wikimedia Commons; (CCA-SA4.0 International license) pp. 28-29 ABB Photo/Shutterstock.com; p. 32 DEA/G. Dagli Orti/De Agostini/Getty Images; pp. 34-35 Maveric149/File: Saqqara - Pyramid of Djoser - entrance to mortuary temple.JPG/Wikimedia Commons; (CCA-SA 3.0 Unported license) pp. 38-39 Leonid Andronov/Shutterstock.com; pp. 44-45 Trazos sobre Papel/Shutterstock.com; p. 47 Bertl123/Shutterstock.com; pp. 54-55 Bruce Yuanyue Bi/Lonely Planet Images/Getty Images; p. 56 Marcus Qwertyus/File: Wainwright Building - 2012. JPG/Wikimedia Commons; (CCA-SA 3.0 Unported license) p. 64 meunierd/Shutterstock.com; p. 66 Tom Ravenscroft/http://www.flickr.com/photos/43391993@N03/4114883611/File: Seagram Building-NewYork-1.jpg/Wikimedia Commons; (CCA 2.0 Generic license) p. 70 Andrewglaser/File: Heliotrop Freiburg.jpg/Wikimedia Commons; (CCA-SA 3.0 Unported license) p. 73 Hedrich Blessing Collection/Chicago History Museum/Archive Photos/Getty Images; p. 75 © Arcaid Images/Alamy Stock Photo; pp. 78-79 Boyd Norton, 1936-, Photographer (NARA record: 1111093 (https://research.archives.gov/person/1111093)/U.S. National Archives and Records Administration/File: SOLAR HEATING AND COOLING DEMONSTRATION PROJECT, WHIC...SCIENCE FOUNDATION - NARA - 557330.jpg/Wikimedia Commons; (Public Domain) pp. 84-85 Cloud Mine Amsterdam/Shutterstock.com; pp. 88-89 Olga Kashubin/Shutterstock.com; p. 91 */Kyodo/Newscom; pp. 94-95 Awakening/Getty Images.

Printed in the United States of America

CONTENTS

INTRODUCTION: More Than Simply Shelter

From temporary camps built by early nomads to temporary buildings designed to house disaster victims, from simple houses built by local craftsmen from local materials in local styles to Frank Gehry's fantastical computer-aided designs, what we build has always been shaped by both what we know and what we believe. As we invent new tools, new technology, and new materials, the physical possibilities of what we can build expand. At the same time, buildings have always been about more than just shelter. A building's size and shape tell us how a culture defines family, social structure, and sometimes the very shape of the cosmos.

In this book, we will not only follow the story of how people built houses, temples, palaces, cathedrals, and skyscrapers, but we will try to understand why they chose to build them.

We begin with the shelters created by early humans, who built temporary dwellings from whatever materials were available as they moved from place to place in search of food. Perhaps these shelters can be better described as semipermanent. Even the earliest known camp, built three hundred thousand years ago on what is now the French Riviera, provides evidence that our ancient ancestors returned to the same place year after year, building the same type of structures on the same site.

Semipermanent camps became permanent settlements around 9000 BCE, when people in the Middle East learned to farm. Permanent versions of nomadic campsites grew into small towns. As populations grew and social organizations became more complex, small towns grew into the first cities, located on the fertile land between the Tigris and Euphrates Rivers.

In the first permanent settlements, people built small houses behind strong walls. Over time, they learned to make bricks from mud and straw—architecture's first major technical breakthrough. As societies grew more complicated, people created new types of buildings to fill new needs. The city-states of Mesopotamia built magnificent homes for kings and gods, creating monumental structures with little more than mud brick. Europe's Bronze Age cultures built tombs and temples with enormous stones, sometimes transporting them across many miles. The ancient Egyptians learned to cut stone into exact shapes and fit them together into smooth walls, creating what they believed would be eternal stone monuments for their rulers and temples for their gods. Whether built in brick or stone, the monumental buildings of the ancient world were the products of complex societies that were able to organize large amounts of manpower and willing to commit the resources to build structures that would embody a society's central ideology.

When we reach the time of the Roman Empire, we find new kinds of public buildings, built with a new material, concrete. Thanks to the invention of the **arch**, and its relatives the **vault** and the **dome**, people could construct buildings with large interior spaces for the first time—spaces in which Roman citizens could congregate to worship their gods, transact their business, or conduct their social lives. In addition to palaces and temples, they built public baths, public halls, amphitheaters, and arenas. As

No matter the shape, style, or size, buildings have always been about more than just shelter.

they expanded, they built Roman towns with distinctively Roman buildings across an empire that stretched at its height from Britain to Egypt.

The next major technological advance we consider occurred in the nineteenth century, when new ways to make iron, steel, and glass made it possible to construct a new type of building: the skyscraper. For centuries, the highest structure in any town or city was the tower on a church, mosque, or temple. Stone and brick walls needed to be strong enough to support the weight of the building above them. Building with prefabricated iron rods and plate glass meant weight was no longer a consideration. Buildings could soar into the air. The first true skyscraper was built in Chicago in 1884. Others soon followed. The first architects to build skyscrapers, known as the Chicago school, designed buildings that explored the possibilities of the form. Taking the motto "form follows function," they created buildings in which the facade reflected the hidden structural frame.

Over the course of the twentieth century, the skyscraper took many forms. In the 1920s and 1930s, American architects encased functional steel frames with decorative facades, while European architects took the first bold steps toward the minimalist aesthetic of the international style, which would come to dominate urban skylines after the Second World War. By the late 1960s, "less is more" had become "less is bore." Neomodernists, postmodernists, deconstructionists and advocates of high-tech style reinvented the skyscraper. Only the steel frame remained constant.

From skyscrapers, we turn to what seemed like the architectural lunatic fringe for much of the twentieth century. In the 1930s and 1940s, while modernist architects built glass-and-steel skyscrapers, a few architects and engineers experimented with the idea of heating homes with solar energy. For the most part, the first solar houses were small and horizontal. The one thing they had in common with skyscrapers was the use of glass.

Inspired originally by the scarcities of the Depression and fuel rationing in World War II, interest in solar houses was closely tied to the availability of fuel throughout the twentieth century. When energy was cheap and plentiful in the 1950s and 1960s, only environmental activists were interested in solar power. The OPEC oil embargo of 1973 brought solar power back into the political and scientific mainstream for a brief time, but when the embargo ended, solar energy became the domain of environmental activists once more. Today, solar energy is only one of the tools architects are using to design environmentally friendly buildings.

The rate of change is faster than it has ever been before, and many of these technological advances, like concrete or solar cells, have important uses beyond architecture. We end by looking at the new technology, new materials, and new ideas that drive building design today, and considering what they may mean for architecture tomorrow.

Early humans in the Ukraine built semipermanent shelters for their winter camps from mammoth bones.

CHAPTER 1
From the First Shelters to the First Cities

From the very beginning, humans have built shelters to protect themselves—from blazing heat, powerful winds, arctic cold, and from dangerous animals and other humans. Historically, the forms those shelters took depended on what materials were available and on the threats presented by the local environment. Inhabitants of the hot, dry climates of Africa's Great Rift Valley or the American Southwest created different shelters from those built in northern Europe or the Arctic Circle. In areas where trees were plentiful, people built wooden frames and covered them with plant materials, matting, cloth, bark, turf, or animal hides. In parts of the world where wood was scarce, they made walls from mud, **fieldstone**, sod, or blocks of snow and ice.

When temporary shelters evolved into permanent dwellings, different cultures created buildings that reflected local conditions not just in their construction material but in their form. In places that suffered from heavy rain or snow, people constructed buildings with pitched roofs so water would run off and snow would not build up. In cold climates, houses often centered around a hearth, with insulated walls to keep the heat in and the wind out. Inhabitants of the tropics constructed buildings using lightweight materials that would allow the most air movement possible. In semiarid regions, thick mud walls with small windows kept out the summer's heat. People built houses on stilts in areas that flooded or suffered from extreme tides. They used light, flexible materials in regions that suffered from frequent earthquakes and cyclones. They even carved out entire underground communities in regions like Cappadocia in Turkey, where the rock was relatively soft and the primary danger came from hostile neighbors instead of a hostile environment.

There is one thing all human shelters have in common: human ingenuity.

NOMADIC SHELTERS

The earliest humans were nomads, who foraged for wild grains and other vegetation and followed the herds of animals that formed a large part of their diet. Sometimes they took advantage of the natural shelter provided by caves and rock ledges. But such shelter was not always available and not always safe: cave bears and other wild predators competed with humans for these natural shelters. More often, nomadic peoples made camp near water and built temporary shelters from the materials at hand.

The earliest known example of such a camp is the Terra Amata site in southern France, where nomadic hunters built shelters three hundred thousand years ago during the Paleolithic period, which is sometimes called the Old Stone Age. Discovered by construction workers in 1965 and excavated by archaeologist Henry de Lumley, the site includes the remains of eleven huts. Rings of post holes surrounded by concentric rings of stones tell us each hut was a long oval, ranging from 26 to 49 feet (7.9 to 14.9 meters) long and from 13 to 20 feet (4 to 6 m) in width—roughly the size of a modern motor home. The people who camped at Terra Amata built these huts using a type of construction known as a palisade wall. They drove stakes—

defensive walls, built of rubble mortared together with mud. The most well known of these fortified hill towns is the multilayered site of Jericho, also known as Tel es-Sultan, located in the Palestinian West Bank.

Although its fortunes have fallen and risen over the centuries, Jericho may be the oldest continuously occupied place in the world. Archaeologists have identified as many as twenty successive settlements at Jericho, beginning with the remains of a nomadic campsite. The earliest permanent houses at Jericho were built with clay lumps the size of baseballs—predecessors of the mud bricks that would become the literal building blocks of architecture throughout the ancient world. By 8000 BCE, Jericho had grown into a fortified town with a defensive exterior wall, strengthened by a massive tower built of rubble and mud. The town was home to between two and three thousand people, who lived in beehive-shaped houses that were built halfway underground and were accessed by wooden steps from the roof. Builders progressed from clay lumps to the first true bricks, which they shaped by hand from clay and water, mixed with a binding material such as straw or reeds, and dried in the sun.

Over the course of a thousand years, houses in Jericho changed from circular one-room dwellings to rectangular rooms arranged around a central courtyard, a design still common in the Middle East today. Bricks changed their shape from oval to rectangular. For the first time, the mud floors and interior walls of houses were "plastered" with a smooth finish of liquid mud. One feature of Jericho from this period suggests its inhabitants designed their houses with more than simple shelter in mind. They covered human skulls with individually modeled plaster faces with pieces of seashells for eyes and displayed the decorated skulls in their homes. They buried the headless bodies under the floor. We don't know why, though some experts suggest this might have been a form of ancestor veneration. Another explanation is the heads might have been trophies of a defeated enemy. While we may never be able to explain these decorations with certainty, we do know that for the people who displayed these skulls, home was more than just protection against wind and rain.

MESOPOTAMIA: The BIRTHPLACE of CIVILIZATION and ARCHITECTURE

Over time, agriculture spread, and permanent settlements followed increasing crop yields. This led to larger populations in the towns, more specialized craftsmen, the beginning of long-distance trade, the rise of a ruling class, and the development of organized religion. Between 4500 and 4000 BCE, the first true cities appeared in Mesopotamia, the fertile land between the Tigris and Euphrates Rivers—now modern Iraq. Mesopotamia's city-states were politically independent but united by a shared culture. The city-states were small by modern standards (they were similar in size to Duluth, Minnesota, or Ashville, North Carolina), yet their culture survived for almost four thousand years through three successive civilizations: Sumer, Babylonia, and Assyria. The more complex social organization of urban culture brought with it the need for new types of buildings: magnificent homes for kings and gods.

Mesopotamia was an unlikely place to produce monumental architecture. The region had little stone or timber. The most readily available building materials were clay, river-grown reeds, and **bitumen**, a naturally occurring asphalt-like substance that seeps to Earth's surface in Iraq.

The poorest Mesopotamians built houses from reeds, using a construction technique very like the one used by the nomadic builders of Terra Amata. They packed bundles of reeds into post holes, then bent them over and tied them together at the top to create a roof frame, which they covered with reed mats.

Bricks made from the region's clay soil were the primary building material. The shape of Mesopotamian bricks changed over the centuries; the basic method for making and using bricks did not. The most common bricks were sun-dried, not that different from the bricks used in Jericho several thousand years earlier. Mesopotamian builders mixed clay from the riverbanks with finely chopped straw and packed the mixture into small wooden molds, which they later removed so the bricks could dry on the ground in hot sun. Sun-dried bricks were made in the summer, when the sun was at its hottest; in fact, the ancient Mesopotamians called the first month of summer "the month of bricks." Sun-dried bricks were cheap to make and easy to replace, but they were easily damaged by the winter rains and the spring floods, when the Tigris and Euphrates escaped their banks and enriched the region's fields with the rich alluvial soil that made the region the "Fertile Crescent." Bricks baked in a kiln were less porous and consequently more durable, but the cost of heating ovens in a country with little wood made kiln-fired bricks very expensive. Because kiln-dried bricks were so expensive, Mesopotamians only used them for the exterior layer of important buildings.

Like the fortified hill towns of ancient Palestine, the Mesopotamian city-states guarded their wealth and their people behind massive defensive walls. For instance, two walls of brick, with rubble packed in between, surrounded the city of Babylon. The exterior wall alone was between 20 and 25 feet (6 to 7.6 m) thick. Within those walls, the city dwellers built their small houses and shops close together, both for structural support and to keep the hot sun off the winding streets below. At the heart of each city stood something new: a walled temple complex. A city might have temples dedicated to many gods, but the largest and most imposing temple would be dedicated to the patron god or goddess of a city. In the city of Ur, for example, the complex included five temples. The largest was dedicated to the moon god, Nanna; one of the smaller temples was dedicated to his spouse, the goddess Ningal. In addition to temples, the complex included palaces, administrative buildings from which rulers and priests governed the city-state, royal storehouses, and workshops owned by the temples. It was both a religious compound and the administrative center of the city-state.

The heart of the temple complex—and the most distinctive architectural creation of ancient Mesopotamia—was not the temple but the **ziggurat**: a multilayered wedding cake of a building intended as a link between the heavens and the earth. The name comes from an Akkadian word meaning "peak" or "high place," and in fact, ziggurats must have looked like artificial mountains on the flat plains of Mesopotamia. Each ziggurat was made up of a stacked set of between three and seven rectangular platforms with sloped walls and a series of steps and ramps that archaeologists believe led to a shrine at the top dedicated to the city's patron god.

The ruins of more than thirty ziggurats have been found to date. The best-preserved ziggurat is also one of the oldest. It stands at Ur, one of the most important Mesopotamian cites, and dates from the third millennium BCE. It appears to have consisted of three platforms, the base of which measures 145 feet (44 m) by 190 feet (58 m) and stands 50 feet (15.2 m) high, the height of an average five-story

The remains of the ziggurat of Ur, which once had three platforms and stood as high as a five-story building

NEBUCHADNEZZAR REBUILDS BABYLON

Nebuchadnezzar II (circa 630–561 BCE) is the most famous of the Mesopotamian kings. Today he is best known from the Biblical account of his military campaign against Jerusalem. From the Babylonian perspective, Nebuchadnezzar was a great ruler and successful general who restored his kingdom to its former glory after years of oppression at the hands of the Assyrians. He was also an ambitious builder who commissioned public building projects in thirteen Mesopotamian cities.

The central focus of his building program was Babylon, the capital city, which he turned into a showplace of the ancient world. He rebuilt its fortifications and enlarged its palace. According to Greek historian Herodotus (ca. 484–425 BCE), Nebuchadnezzar built an enormous seven-story ziggurat to honor the kingdom's primary god, Marduk, each level covered with a different color of glazed brick. The most famous of his improvements are the grand processional boulevard and gateway that led to the city's sacred compound. The boulevard was ornamented with 120 lions in glazed brick relief against a background of deep blue glazed brick and paved with red and yellow stones, each engraved with a prayer from Nebuchadnezzar to Marduk; the Ishtar Gate was similarly decorated with golden bulls and dragons, symbols of the city's primary gods.

Some scholars believe Nebuchadnezzar also created the Hanging Gardens of Babylon—an enormous pyramid of vaulted terraces that was considered one of the seven wonders of the ancient world—to comfort his young wife, who missed the green hills of her Iranian homeland.

As part of Babylon's city wall, the Ishtar Gate was once considered one of the seven wonders of the ancient world.

building. The center of the ziggurat is a core of sun-dried brick, laid in mortar, a paste made of liquid clay or bitumen that bonds the bricks together. Builders placed woven reed mats between the layers of brick, which may have acted as a system to drain water out of the walls. The central core was covered with a layer of kiln-dried brick, 8 feet (2.4 m) thick, which was more weather resistant than the material used at the core. Written accounts of later ziggurats suggest that each level would have been painted a different color, with the shrine at the top clad in glistening glazed brick.

Because ancient Mesopotamians built using mud brick, which is fragile and requires regular maintenance, little of their architecture remains except the foundations. Nonetheless, the decorative fragments that remain hint at their former splendor: a coating of white gypsum plaster that must have shimmered in the sun, mosaics of colored stones and mother of pearl, and, in the case of Nebuchadnezzar's Babylon, multicolored glazed bricks in the same colors that would be used later to decorate Islamic palaces and mosques in the same region.

MUD-BRICK BUILDINGS in OTHER TIMES and PLACES

Building with sunbaked mud bricks was not limited to the *tel* cultures of the Middle East and the ancient civilizations of Mesopotamia. In Eurasia and Africa, the growth of towns followed the spread of agriculture. Mud bricks became a favorite building material throughout the Mediterranean basin and beyond. Archaeologists have uncovered settlements built with mud brick at Çatal Hüyuk (ca. 6500–5700 BCE) in western Turkey, in ruins on Crete that date from 5000 BCE, in the cities of the Indus Valley civilization (ca. 3000–1300 BCE) in what is now Pakistan, and in those of the Longshan culture of ancient China (ca. 3000–1900 BCE). In the Americas, the Peruvian city of Chan Chan (ca. 850–1470 CE) and the distinctive pueblos of the Anasazi in the American Southwest were both built using sunbaked mud bricks. Today, adobe—a Spanish corruption of *al-tub*, the Arabic word for sun-dried mud bricks, which is itself derived from the ancient Egyptian word for mud—remains a popular construction technique in semiarid regions across the world, used for the humblest of homes and monumental mosques alike. The details varied from culture to culture, but the basic construction technique remained the same: mud, water, straw and sun.

Sun-dried bricks are one of mankind's oldest construction methods, but as the ruins of ancient Mesopotamia make clear, they aren't the best choice for building long term. When ancient humans wanted to build for eternity, they chose stone.

Prehistoric inhabitants of Skara Brae in Orkney built houses using slabs of fieldstone for walls and furniture.

CHAPTER 2
Stone Walls

Unlike buildings made of wood, reeds, or mud bricks, stone buildings last. Even when a building falls, the stones themselves can be reused—and they often were.

FIELDSTONE WALLS

Rough fieldstone—literally the rocks removed from a field when it is prepared for farming—was one of our earliest building materials. The inhabitants of the ancient city of Jericho, for instance, used fieldstone to build their defensive walls. Like reeds, ice blocks, or clay lumps, fieldstone was used for building because it was readily available. For the most part, people used fieldstone in the condition in which they found it, making little or no attempt to change its natural shape or surface. Sometimes builders laid the stone in horizontal layers of roughly the same height, called courses. Sometimes they built "uncoursed" walls in which rocks are laid in uneven rows, also described as "random rubble walls." Sometimes they set stones in a wall with clay mortar or bitumen. Sometimes they "dry-set" the stones, arranging them in such a way that vertical pressure held them in place.

A dramatic example of early fieldstone walls can be found at Skara Brae, a Neolithic village in the Orkney

Islands off the northern tip of Scotland. Around 3100 BCE, the island's inhabitants built not only small houses but also furniture from thick sandstone slabs. Like other early builders, the people of Skara Brae built their houses partially underground: they dug out pits between 13 and 20 feet (4 to 6 m) across and 10 feet (3 m) deep, which they lined with sandstone to form walls. The sandstone was held together with rubbish rotted down to a sticky consistency that helped stabilize and insulate the walls. Each house centered on a sunken, stone-lined hearth for heating and cooking. We don't know how the roofs were made; some archaeologists speculate that because timber was scarce they used whale ribs covered with hide. Inside the houses, they stacked stone slabs to create storage shelves and larger bins that may have been filled with straw and furs to make beds.

Fieldstone—in courses or uncoursed, set with mortar or dry-set—remained a popular material for **vernacular architecture** through the centuries. Fieldstone fences marked farm boundaries in colonial New England, and fieldstone fireplaces heated log cabins on the American frontier. Builders used fieldstone for foundation walls well into the early twentieth century. Today, fieldstone walls, built with techniques not substantially different than those used by early humans, are still popular design features.

MEGALITHIC MONUMENTS

At much the same time that the people of Skara Brae built their small fieldstone houses, people across Europe built monumental structures using enormous stones called **megaliths**. Like ancient Mesopotamia's mud-brick ziggurats, megalithic construction projects could only be built by a complex society with the ability to organize manpower, first to quarry and transport the stones and then to build the structures. More importantly, a society needed a shared ideology powerful enough to inspire the creation of a structure that demanded an immense expenditure of resources.

Many megalithic structures were not buildings but circles of standing stones, known as "henges." More than one thousand examples of stone circles have been found in the British Isles and Brittany, including the famous examples at Avebury, Stonehenge, and Carnac. The size and number of stones in these circles differ widely. Their purpose and builders are unknown, but the fact that tombs, enclosures, and ceremonial sites surround some of the larger circles, such as Stonehenge, suggests they formed part of a larger ritual complex.

Stone circles weren't the only megalithic monuments built in Neolithic and Bronze Age Europe. The tombs associated with Stonehenge and Avebury are related to a larger tradition of passage tombs, found throughout the coastal and island regions of western Europe from Denmark to the Mediterranean. Passage tombs are mounds built from large stones and then covered with smaller stones or earth. The burial chamber is entered through a narrow, tunnel-like corridor. In the most famous of these, the Irish tomb at Newgrange (ca. 3000 BCE), the interior passage is lined with upright stone slabs, decorated with stylized carved patterns of spirals and concentric circles. The central burial chamber is roofed with flat stone slabs in circular courses, each one set closer to the center to form a beehive-shaped ceiling—a technique known as a corbelled dome.

Bronze Age peoples on the Mediterranean islands of Malta and Gozo used similar construction techniques to build massive stone temple complexes over a period of

An interior hallway in the megalithic passage tomb at Newgrange, Ireland

fifteen hundred years, between 4000 and 2500 BCE. They built the outer shell of each temple from great slabs of hard gray limestone, laid both horizontally and vertically. A softer, paler limestone formed the interior walls, which were decorated with carved spiral motifs, trees, plants, and various animals. Inside each temple, semicircular chambers were laid out symmetrically on either side of a main corridor, creating a cloverleaf-shaped floor plan. The temples at Malta and Gozo are among the most impressive buildings from prehistoric Europe.

All of these structures—from the small stone huts of Skara Brae to the great temples of Gozo—share one common feature: they were built using stone in its natural state. Around 2600 BCE, the ancient Egyptians took an enormous step forward in stone architecture: building with **dressed stone**.

BUILDING for ETERNITY in ANCIENT EGYPT

Egyptian civilization was born on the fertile strips of land that lined the banks of the Nile River from Aswan to the Delta. Unlike their Mesopotamian counterparts, Egyptian builders had ready access to a variety of workable stone: granite quarries at Aswan, limestone on the Giza plain, and sandstone at Gebel Silsila, as well as deposits of basalt, gypsum, alabaster and quartzite.

But Egyptian innovations in working with stone were not the result of availability. If that were the case, they would have used stone for ordinary buildings, like the farmers of Skara Brae. Instead, they built shops, craftsmen's workshops, and the homes of both peasants and noblemen from mud brick. Only official buildings, commissioned by

the pharaohs themselves or the priests who served them, were made of stone. This was partly a matter of logistics: quarrying stone at one location, transporting it by boat and sledge to another, and constructing monumental stone buildings took the labor of thousands of men—men who were available only through government conscription. But it was also a matter of theology. Two fundamental beliefs shaped Egyptian culture: the pharaoh's divinity and the need to provide for life after death. Eternity was the theme that drove Egyptian art and architecture, from the smallest statuette to the Great Pyramids at Giza. The Egyptians built in stone because stone would last forever.

Egypt's first major monuments, built during the First and Second Dynasties (3200–2780 BCE), were mud-brick

Part of Zoser's burial complex at Saqqara, this temple's walls illustrate the new technology of building with dressed stone.

tombs known as mastabas. Mastabas were rectangular structures with sides that sloped inward toward a flat top, built above burial chambers cut through the desert sand and into the bedrock below. Each tomb contained a chapel that held offerings for the deceased to use in the afterlife and a secret room where a statue of the deceased was stored.

In 2650 BCE, the pharaoh Zoser assumed power during an era that was possibly the most brilliant artistic period in pharaonic Egypt. When the time came for him to plan his funeral monument, he wanted something larger and grander than the mastabas of his predecessors.

Zoser's Step Pyramid—built at Saqqara near the capital city of Memphis around 2630 BCE—is generally considered the beginning of true stone architecture. It is the first building we know of that was constructed with stones shaped into precise rectangular blocks and fitted together with minimal joints into a smooth, continuous surface. In earlier stone walls, whether built from fieldstones or megaliths, the shape of each stone can be separately identified. Towering 200 feet (61 m) over a granite-lined burial shaft, the Step Pyramid was built in six immense tiers that were essentially a stack of mastabas made of stone. It was more like a Mesopotamian ziggurat in shape than the classic Egyptian pyramid.

The Step Pyramid stands at the center of a 36-acre (14.6-hectare) complex of monuments. The complex also included temples and eleven separate burial shafts for other members of the royal family. A limestone wall, 1 mile (1.6 kilometers) long and 34 feet (10.4 m) high with thirteen fake doorways in addition to the real entrance, surrounded the complex. It was the site for important religious celebrations during Zoser's lifetime as well as after his death.

In creating Zoser's pyramid, Egyptian builders took designs, details, and techniques previously used in buildings made from wood, reed, and mud brick and rendered them in stone. They set stone blocks in the same mortar pattern they had previously used for brick buildings. They copied the bundles of papyrus reeds that gave added strength to mud-brick walls, creating stone columns—one of later architecture's basic components. The shaft of each column imitated the plant's triangular stem. The block on the top of each shaft, known as the **capital**, was shaped like the open cluster of papyrus flowers or a lotus leaf.

Once begun, stone architecture developed rapidly in Egypt. It took only a few generations for pyramids to acquire their distinctive shape. By the reign of the pharaoh Snefru (ca. 2613–2589 BCE), Egyptians built pyramids and temples using gigantic stone blocks. Around 1500 BCE, they began to build a new style of temple, with larger, more complex covered spaces that were spanned by stone lintels set on a forest of columns. The most famous example is the **hypostyle hall** in the temple at Karnak.

These ambitious building projects required an enormous investment of time and resources. According to Herodotus, it took one hundred thousand men working in three-month shifts twenty years to complete the Great Pyramid of Giza (ca. 2550 BCE). In fact, the men who worked on the pyramid itself made up only a small portion of the effort involved.

Laborers cut hundreds of thousands of massive stone blocks from quarries and transported them downriver. Once the stone-laden boats reached the landing stage, workers transferred the blocks to wooden sledges, which large teams of men pulled to the work site on rollers. At the construction site, more men dragged the stone blocks into place up the sides of the pyramid using specially built ramps made of packed earth and crushed stone. In addition to stone blocks, teams of workers transported hundreds of loads of timber, sand, and Nile mud for every project. Skilled craftsmen produced the tools needed for every step of the job, from the simple stone picks and copper saws used to cut and dress the stone to the enormous boats used to transport it down river.

Every step of the process took manpower. The work season was tied to the Nile's cyclical flooding. A few skilled craftsmen—stonecutters, sculptors and bricklayers—worked on the monuments year round. Most of the workmen, the men who dragged the massive stones from quarry to river bank to building site and onto the pyramids, were farmers who were conscripted to work on the pharaoh's projects for the four months each year when the flooding of the Nile brought work in the fields to a halt. Once conscripted, workers had to be trained, fed, and clothed.

Conscription was a complicated process organized by a second workforce: an army of clerks.

The Egyptians built enormous stone monuments for three thousand years. In the process, Egyptian architects created new architectural elements such as fluted columns, capitals, and colonnades that have influenced Western architecture ever since, beginning with the

Ancient Egyptian builders created the covered space in the hypostyle hall at Saqqara using columns and lintels.

buildings of ancient Greece—a different form of eternity than they expected.

STONE WALLS in OTHER TIMES and PLACES

Monumental architecture using dressed stone developed independently in other parts of the world where there was ready access to stone, a large workforce that could be conscripted by the state or would volunteer for the glory of God, and the willingness to expend valuable resources creating buildings that would embody a society's central ideology. The architects of Hellenistic Greece (323–80 BCE) used stone to create buildings for both civic and religious purposes: theaters, temples, and the public gathering places known as agoras. Beginning in the fifth century CE, masons in the Indian subcontinent built Hindu and Buddhist temples from carved sandstone, creating three-dimensional models of the the sacred diagram of the universe, the

IMHOTEP: The FIRST ARCHITECT

Most architects of the ancient world remain anonymous. We are more apt to know the name of the king who commissioned a building than the man who designed it. In ancient Mesopotamia, for instance, kings had their names impressed in the bricks used in the great buildings they commissioned.

The first architect whose name was recorded was an Egyptian, Imhotep, who was responsible for constructing Zoser's huge funerary complex at Saqqara. He is not only given credit for creating a new way of building stone walls, but also for translating architectural details from less enduring materials into cut stone masonry, replacing their functional purpose with a symbolic one. In recognition of his achievements, Zoser gave Imhotep an honor no artist received before him: a place in history. At Zoser's order, Imhotep's name and titles, including "chief of sculptors," were carved on the base of a statue of the pharaoh.

Today we would call Imhotep a "Renaissance man." In addition to being an innovative architect, he was a scholar, priest, astrologer, magician, and physician. His skill as both an architect and a physician led him to be recognized as a deity. During his lifetime, he was named the son of Ptah, patron god of craftsmen and creator of the universe. Two hundred years after his death, Imhotep was worshipped as the god of medicine in both Egypt and Greece, where he was identified with the Greek god of medicine, Asclepius.

mandala. Artists in Cambodia's Khmer kingdom built the tapering towers and elaborately carved temples of Angkor Wat, still the largest religious monument in the world, over the course of the ninth through the fourteenth centuries. In medieval Europe, beginning in the tenth century, military leaders replaced wooden stockades with stone fortresses, and religious leaders built great stone churches and abbeys, moving from the thick walls, massive pillars, and rounded arches of the Romanesque style to the pointed arches and soaring towers of the Gothic. In the Americas, the Aztecs built stone pyramids and shrines at Tenochtitlán (ca. 1400 CE) and the Mayans built massive stepped pyramids and ornate palaces from limestone from the first to the tenth century CE.

All early builders, whether they worked with timber, mud brick, or stone, shared one common challenge: how to span a space to create a window or doorway, or to build a roof over an enclosed space. The problem would not be solved until the first century BCE, when the Romans invented a new architectural technique: the arch.

The Pont du Gard aqueduct in Nîmes, France, is a marvel of Roman engineering.

CHAPTER 3
The Arch

Structures as different as framed wooden huts, the megalithic tomb at Newgrange, the ancient Egyptian temple at Karnak, and the classical Greek Parthenon all were built using a technique known as **post-and-lintel** construction. In this system, two upright members (the posts) support a third, horizontal member (the lintel).

The width of a space that can be spanned with post-and-lintel construction is limited by the strength of the materials used. Posts require **compressive strength**: they need to be able to support the weight of both a lintel and the walls above it without being crushed or buckling. This is the lesser problem for post-and-lintel construction. Stone and brick posts, in particular, possess enormous compressive strength. The greater problem comes with the lintel, which needs **tensile strength**: it must be able to support its own weight across the opening without breaking, as well as the weight of any walls that rest on it. The farther apart the posts, the greater the chance the lintel will collapse.

Prior to the production of cast-iron columns and girders in the nineteenth century, post-and-lintel construction used stone slabs or stout timbers as lintels. Stone and wood could safely span no more than 10 to 15 feet (3 to 4.6 m) between posts. As a result, the interiors of buildings constructed using post-and-lintel construction were made up of a series

The unknown builders of Stonehenge used post-and-lintel construction to create their stone monuments.

of small, dark rooms, with few or no windows. In order to build larger rooms, like the great hypostyle hall at Karnak, builders created rows of columns (posts) to support the roof beams, leaving little open space in the center of the room.

For many of the structures built in the ancient world, small rooms and no windows were not a problem. Gathering places were not needed inside royal tombs. Only priests and the ruler worshipped inside the shrine at the top of a Mesopotamian ziggurat or an Egyptian temple. Classical Greek theaters and agoras were open-air structures, defined by colonnades rather than roofs.

The ancient Romans constructed the first public buildings designed around grand interior spaces, using a new way of spanning space.

BUILDING on an IMPERIAL SCALE in CLASSICAL ROME

Public buildings served a new purpose in the Roman Empire. Official Roman architecture was designed to express the empire's might. Like other ancient peoples, Romans built palaces and temples, but they also built public baths, bridges, aqueducts, **basilicas** (halls that served as covered markets, courts, and public meeting places), and the amphitheaters and circuses where a growing urban population enjoyed grand public entertainments. The empire's expansion led to the creation of new Roman towns, each of which was built on a grid plan that included room for all of the amenities needed to make Romans comfortable away from Rome.

Romans sought practical solutions to the problems of expanding urban architecture: a way to build distinctively Roman buildings in new cities across an empire that stretched from the Thames to the Nile. The solution to creating architectural unity on an imperial scale in regions with different climates and natural resources turned out to be a flexible new building material, concrete, and a new construction technique, the arch. The basis for vaults and domes, arches made it possible for Roman builders to create covered spaces without interior supporting columns. For the first time, buildings could hold large numbers of people for business, worship, or recreation.

Arches

The arch replaced the column as the basic structural element of Roman architecture.

A true arch is built from a continuous line of wedge-shaped blocks called voussoirs, set in a curve between two vertical elements to span an open distance. A **keystone** at the crown of the curve locks the voussoirs into a stable unit that can support not only itself but any load above it.

All arches transfer the loads they support both downward and outward. The shape of the arch diverts the downward thrust of tensile stress around the arch itself and down the vertical supports. In order to stabilize the competing stresses while an arch was being built, arches were often constructed around a wooden frame that was removed after the keystone was set—a technique known as centering. Once the arch is complete, the blocks are kept in place by the balance between compression and tensile stresses.

A true arch is able to span ten times the distance as a stone lintel set across two columns. In fact, a series of arches, set side by side, can cover many miles. The Romans used arches arranged this way to build sewers, bridges, and most dramatically, aqueducts, such as the Pont du Gard in southern France. By using arches of different heights, Roman engineers could maintain the slope needed to transport water from its source to a town using only gravity. Arched aqueducts carried water to Rome itself from as far as 52 miles (84 km) away.

Vaults

Expanding the form of the arch creates vaults and domes. They share the arch's structural advantages but present new challenges to the builder.

When multiple arches are placed next to each other in a row, they become a barrel vault, a curved ceiling over two parallel walls. When barrel vaults are combined, they can support multiple stories of masonry. The Colosseum in Rome is an excellent example of this. The enormous amphitheater in central Rome is big enough to hold 140 high-school gyms. The structure rests on two systems of barrel-vaulted corridors at the ground level: four concentric corridors circled the central arena, and eighty hallways intersected with them, fanning out from the arena in rays. Above the ground level, additional vaults led to the Colosseum's seating sections. This system allowed smooth traffic in and out of the arena.

The major problem with the barrel vault is that it is impossible to put windows in the walls because the downward and outward thrust of continuous arches needs the support of thick, solid walls. The cross or groin vault, formed when two barrel vaults intersect at right angles, solved this problem. The edges formed where the vaults meet, called groins, transfer the weight of the vault to pillars at the four corners of the vault. The walls between the pillars are not load bearing, making it possible to cut windows or doors in them. One of the earliest examples of a groin vault is the Basilica Nova in Rome (begun 307 CE), in which the central space is composed of three bays roofed by cross vaults and lit by windows that fill the intersection between the vaults and the side and end walls.

Domes

Rotating an arch 360 degrees around a central axis creates a dome.

Domes can cover an enormous amount of interior space, but they offer a new engineering challenge: the lateral thrust known as "hoop stress." This refers to the fact that the blocks in a dome thrust outward, the way a balloon bulges if you compress it from above. The bigger the dome, the more liable it is to crack or collapse as a result of hoop stress. Over the centuries, architects have stabilized domes with vertical ribs inside the dome, horizontal "tension rings" buried inside the masonry, and external **buttresses**—projecting structures that support a load-bearing wall by absorbing the hoop stress.

The Romans used domes as roofs for temples, basilicas, and even bathhouses. The most important Roman building with a dome is the Pantheon, a temple that is considered the crowning achievement of Roman architecture. Built during the reign of the emperor Augustus (27 BCE–14 CE) and rebuilt between 120 and 125 CE, under the reign of the emperor Hadrian, the Pantheon is a masterpiece of arches, vaults, and a single massive dome. Made with 5,000 tons (4,500 metric tons) of concrete, the Pantheon's dome is supported on sixteen barrel vaults that spread the weight to eight concrete piers, which are disguised with ornamental columns.

The builders used several different techniques to lighten the dome's weight as it rose higher. They created different concrete formulas for different layers, from heavy basalt in the bottom layers through lightweight pumice to empty clay bottles at the top. They made the walls progressively thinner, from 23 feet (7 m) at the base to 2 feet (0.6 m) at the top. And they shaped the concrete into a honeycomb pattern known as **coffering**. This not only helped reduce the dome's weight, it also produces the illusion that the dome floats above the drum wall that supports it. At the dome's center, a round opening 30 feet (9 meters) wide, called an oculus, provides the only natural light in the building.

The Pantheon became an essential stop for tourists during the heyday of the Roman Empire and remains one today. The building's dome is impressive in part because of its size. It remained the largest dome in the world until the development of iron and reinforced concrete in the second half of the nineteenth century. The Pantheon's dome is no longer the largest in the world, but it is still an architectural marvel thanks to its perfect proportions: the diameter of the dome is exactly equal to the height from the floor to the oculus. If the dome were doubled, it would form a perfect sphere that would fill the rotunda and touch the floor.

The POINTED ARCH and GOTHIC ARCHITECTURE

The arch joined the column as a basic element that would be used by architects in many times and places, both for structural support and decoration. Over time, different styles of arches came to define specific architectural styles, including the pointed arch of Gothic architecture and the horseshoe arch of the Islamic world.

The pointed arch was more than a stylistic device. It was a critical structural element in the Gothic cathedrals of the late medieval world.

Early medieval churches were built in the Romanesque style. As their name makes clear, such churches borrowed from the architecture of the Roman Empire. Romanesque buildings were a variation on the Roman basilica, with thick stone walls, massive pillars, and rounded arches.

FILIPPO BRUNELLESCHI'S DOME

The Duomo of Florence is considered the greatest architectural achievement of the Italian Renaissance. Begun in 1296 by Arnolfo di Cambio, Florence's cathedral was under construction for 150 years. It was 1420 before the council responsible for constructing the cathedral approved a plan for completing the huge dome that tops the cathedral, after setting up a contest soliciting ideas two years earlier. The original design called for an enormous dome built using stone rings buried in its masonry rather than external buttresses. The ideal was a dome that would rise above the cathedral with no visible means of support, like the Roman Pantheon.

The man who won the competition, Filippo Brunelleschi (1377–1446), was a goldsmith by training, like many other Renaissance artists and architects. Brunelleschi had spent years measuring classical Greek and Roman monuments; he used those lessons in designing the Duomo. In addition to the internal rings called for in the original design, Brunelleschi devised several other ways to control hoop stress in the dome. He invented an inner and outer dome, supported by eight large ribs, reducing the weight the structure had to support. He built the lower part of the dome with stone blocks, but he constructed the upper half from bricks laid in an interlocking herringbone pattern. The complex pattern meant the bricks bore their own weight at each stage of construction, so the usual expensive central supports were not needed.

In addition to his work on the Duomo, Brunelleschi is known for rediscovering the science of perspective, which allows artists to realistically draw three-dimensional objects on a two-dimensional page.

The Basilica of St. Denis was the first Gothic cathedral, a style defined by pointed arches and ribbed vaults.

In the late eleventh century CE, the first European Crusaders returned from the Middle East, bringing with them not only luxury goods but new forms of knowledge, including the pointed arch, which Islamic architects had developed as early as the seventh century CE. Visually, pointed arches contribute to the sense of upward movement that is central to the Gothic style. Structurally, pointed arches are more flexible than their rounded counterparts. Arches of the same height can span different distances by varying the angle of the arch. That meant that, unlike groin vaults, "rib vaults" could be built on a base of any shape by making the arches narrower or wider. Vaults built using pointed arches are supported by a framework of diagonal stone ribs, made by the intersection of the arches. Because the weight of the vault moved diagonally through the arched ribs across each bay instead of resting on the vault walls, rib vaults could extend upward—making good the visual promise of upward movement suggested by the form of the arches.

When French churchman Abbot Suger (1081–1151) decided to remodel the Basilica of St. Denis (1135–1144), he replaced the heavy walls and small windows of the existing Romanesque structure with a soaring, light-filled space based on the pointed arch and the rib vault. The rigidity of the rib vaults allowed him to replace small windows in stone walls with magnificent stained glass, including the first rose window. His intention was to have the physical church reflect his theological belief that man can contemplate God through material glory. The result was the first Gothic church.

Suger's renovation provided the pattern for Gothic cathedrals. Over the next fifty years, cathedrals in Suger's Gothic style appeared in cities all across Europe, each one larger and lighter than the last. With the invention of the **flying buttress**—half arches applied to the exterior of the building that counteracted the lateral thrust of the interior rib vaults—Gothic architects moved structural support from the interior to the exterior of the building, allowing them to construct higher buildings with thinner walls that could become tracery settings for ever larger stained-glass windows.

Gothic architects transformed the structure of their buildings from the solid masonry of Roman construction to a skeleton covered with a non-load-bearing wall, known as a **curtain wall**, but the height of their soaring cathedrals was still limited by the need for massive load-bearing structures at the ground level. That limitation would not be overcome until the Industrial Revolution brought more advanced ways of making iron, steel, and glass in the nineteenth century.

Louis Sullivan's Wainwright Building epitomized his idea that "form follows function."

CHAPTER 4
The Structural Steel Frame

For centuries the height of buildings was limited by the ability of walls to support not only their own weight, but that of the floors above them. Stone and brick buildings, in particular, required massive structures with load-bearing walls. The higher the building, the thicker the walls at its base.

CRYSTAL PALACES

In the mid-nineteenth century, the development of the iron and steel industries and new techniques of glass manufacturing made it possible to build new types of buildings using prefabricated iron rods and sheets of glass. It was a good way to construct buildings that needed to be large, strong, and full of natural light. Buildings made this way could go up quickly, especially compared to buildings made from brick or stone.

At first, this new technology was used for buildings no one considered "architecture," such as factories, covered markets, and railroad stations. In 1851, the Great Exhibition of the Works of Industry of All Nations in London, nicknamed the Crystal Palace Exhibition, changed the public's perception that iron and glass construction was utilitarian. The exhibition was housed in a giant glass and steel building designed for the purpose

MR. EIFFEL'S TOWER

The Eiffel Tower was intended to be a temporary installation, built for the Paris World's Fair of 1889, which celebrated the one-hundredth anniversary of the French Revolution.

More than one hundred artists submitted plans to build a monument on the Champs-de-Mars at the entrance to the exhibition. French bridge engineer and metals expert Alexandre Gustave Eiffel (1832–1923)—who also designed the internal structure for the Statue of Liberty—won the commission with his design for a wrought iron tower.

Eiffel's previous designs were noted for their lightness, grace, and strength. Those same qualities are evident in his design for the Eiffel Tower. The plan called for more than 18,000 wrought iron pieces and 2.5 million rivets to be assembled in an open-latticework tower on a 4-acre (1.6 ha) base of reinforced concrete. Four piers curved upward and converged at the top, punctuated by two platforms that provided the tower with structural stability and gave exhibition goers a vantage point from which to view the city below them. Despite its lacy appearance, the only elements of the tower that do not contribute to its structural integrity are the grillwork arches that link the bases together, which Eiffel added to reassure visitors the structure was safe.

On March 31, 1889, with the last rivet in place, Eiffel climbed the 1,710 steps to the top and unfurled the French flag. Eiffel's tower rose 986 feet (300.5 m) into the sky, making it the tallest building in the world.

The tower earned Eiffel the nickname "magician of iron."

by Sir Joseph Paxton (1801–1865), a gardener whose previous design experience was limited to greenhouses for the Duke of Devonshire. At the time, the Crystal Palace was the largest covered interior ever built: nearly 1 million square feet (92,900 square meters) of exhibit halls, built on three levels, with a semicircular atrium that rose to a height of 108 feet (33 m). Essentially a giant greenhouse, its framework of cast-iron columns and girders was built with parts prefabricated in Birmingham and mounted with standardized panes of glass.

The exhibition drew over six million visitors between May 1 and October 15—visitors who were as amazed by the nearly transparent building as by the exhibits it housed. But the Crystal Palace's popularity wasn't universal. The building was ridiculed in popular magazines like *Punch* and reviled by critics like John Ruskin, who derided it as "a cucumber frame."

It would be almost one hundred years before building with steel and glass was an accepted architectural practice.

CHICAGO REACHES for the SKY

The technology of building with cast-iron frames found a new use in Chicago at the end of the nineteenth century.

The city was growing rapidly thanks to its critical location as a transportation hub between eastern industry and western agriculture. There was little room for Chicago's business district to expand. The city's downtown was hemmed in by Lake Michigan, the Chicago River, and a tangle of railroads—the same factors that contributed to its growth. The only direction in which to build was up.

Chicago's earliest tall buildings still depended in part on load-bearing masonry walls, which required thickened

"FORM FOLLOWS FUNCTION"

Chicago architect Louis Sullivan (1856–1924) was the first to grasp the aesthetic possibilities of the new technology, which he laid out in an article called "The Tall Office Building Artistically Considered" in 1896. Declaring that "form follows function," he designed buildings that emphasized their height and the lightness of their frames. His buildings expressed the "loftiness" of the skyscraper, which he felt should be "a proud and soaring thing." He treated each building as if it were a classical column, with a base, shaft, and capital. Unlike the modernists of the mid-twentieth century, who adopted "form follows function" as a prescription for minimalism, Sullivan did not reject ornamentation. Instead, he believed American architects should invent their own kind of ornament rather than relying on European models. His lush, often romantic ornamentation focused around entrances, the panels between windows, and cornices. It seemed to grow organically from the simple form of his buildings.

Sullivan demonstrated his design principles in the Wainwright Building (1890). Commissioned by St. Louis brewer Ellis Wainwright, the exterior of the ten-story structure reflects its interior organization, even though the steel structure itself is not visible. Sullivan treated the facade as a grid of horizontal and vertical lines. Horizontal bays of windows stretch across the building, separated by fluted vertical members that connect the building's base and cornice. Heavier vertical piers at each corner articulate the building's height and, together with the ornate frieze under the cornice, create a frame for the grid.

bases to support the weight of additional floors. A new solution came about almost by accident in 1884, when a bricklayer's strike brought construction of the ten-story Home Insurance Building to a halt. Architect William LeBaron Jenney responded by designing a structural frame of steel and iron girders, the same technology Paxton used to build the Crystal Palace. When the strike ended, Jenney installed a curtain wall on the steel frame: a masonry wall with no load-bearing function. The result was a building that weighed two-thirds less than a similarly sized building made of solid masonry. People were so worried the building would collapse that the city halted its construction until they could investigate whether it was structurally sound.

The combination of steel frame and curtain wall launched a new type of building: the skyscraper. Buildings could be taller, with larger interior spaces. Walls could be thinner. Lighter frames meant architects no longer needed to minimize doors and windows to maintain the structural integrity of walls. The group of architects and engineers who became known as the Chicago school—including Daniel Burnham, John Wellborn Root, Dankmar Adler, and Louis Sullivan—took full advantage of the new possibilities, designing utilitarian, multistoried commercial buildings with exteriors that reflected their structural frames and emphasized their verticality.

GOING UP?

Skyscrapers required more than thinner walls and lighter materials. Luckily, one of the main innovations needed to establish the skyscraper as a viable building form already existed: Elisha Otis's elevator brake.

Elisha Otis (1811–1861), the man who made elevators safe, was a tinkerer who liked to make things work better. He moved from job to job, inventing labor-saving devices as he went: a better turbine for a water-powered mill, an automatic bread oven, a faster train brake. In 1852, a group of investors hired him to convert a sawmill into a bedstead factory. When he got to the factory, he realized he would need a hoist to lift machinery to the upper floors.

Power hoists were nothing new. The first power hoist was introduced in a British cotton mill in 1830. By the 1850s, several American factories used steam-powered elevators to move material and machinery, but no one considered using them to move people because they were prone to failure. Often a rope broke, sending the elevator cab into free fall. Existing safety devices required an operator to keep his head and activate the device—hard to do when the elevator cab was hurtling toward the ground.

Once again, Otis was inspired to build something better: an automatic safety device to prevent the elevator cab from falling if the hoist rope broke. Drawing on his brief experience building carriages and wagons, he built a device that clamped onto the vertical rails on which the cab moved if the hoist rope lost tension.

When the bedstead factory failed the following year, Otis opened a small elevator factory. He sold his first freight elevator on September 20, 1853. Despite a quick first sale, business was slow initially. Sales picked up after Otis agreed to demonstrate the machine at the second New York World's Fair, held in May 1854. P. T. Barnum turned Otis's elevator into a crowd-pleasing stunt. Once an hour, Otis rode his elevator to the top, where he took out a saber and slashed through the hoist ropes. Crowds screamed as the elevator dropped and cheered as the safety brake jerked it to a halt after a few seconds. Otis would sweep off his hat, bow to the crowd, and announce "All safe, ladies and gentlemen, all safe." It was a brilliant way to promote the safety elevator. By 1856, Otis had installed fifty-three freight elevators.

In 1857, Otis installed his first passenger elevator in the New York department store E.V. Haughwout & Co. The steam-powered elevator climbed the store's five stories in less than a minute. Thirty years later, Otis elevators provided the vertical transportation needed to make a ten- or twelve- or fifty-story building practical.

Today, more than 1.4 million Otis elevators operate in buildings around the world.

The GOLDEN AGE of SKYSCRAPERS

With the second generation of tall buildings, American architects turned their back on Sullivan's idea that "form follows function" and returned to more traditional architecture, encasing functional steel frames with decorative facades based on a variety of styles. Some architects looked to the past for design inspiration, borrowing details from Gothic cathedrals, Greek temples, and Renaissance palaces. Others rejected revivalist styles and instead featured industrial materials such as steel, chrome and glass, combining industry, modernity, and luxury in a style known as art deco. For example, architect William Van Alen included fenders, hood ornaments, and hubcaps in the design of the Chrysler Building (1930) because the owner, Walter P. Chrysler, wanted his skyscraper to celebrate the automobiles his company manufactured.

Chicago-school buildings emphasized their verticality; the next generation of skyscrapers was unabashedly built to be tall. Chrysler, for instance, asked Van Alen to design a building taller than the Eiffel Tower, then the tallest structure in the world. For a time, it looked like the Chrysler Building might lose the title of tallest building

New York's Chrysler Building is a leading example of art deco design.

to the Bank of Manhattan Trust Company before it was completed, but Van Alen had a trick up his sleeve. The workmen constructed the famous 185-foot (56.4 m) needle-thin spire that tops the Chrysler Building in secret, building it inside the structure. Van Alen waited until the last possible minute to install the spire, making the Chrysler Building taller than its rival by the 185 feet of the spire. It was a short-lived victory. The Chrysler Building was the tallest building in the world only until the Empire State Building was completed four months later.

"LESS IS MORE"

In the 1920s and 1930s, adherents of the idea that "form follows function" could be found in Europe rather than in the United States. Dutch architect Gerrit Rietveld (1888–1964) applied cubist principles to houses, emphasizing rectangular shapes, primary colors, and projecting horizontal planes. In France, Le Corbusier (1887–1965) experimented with unadorned concrete, combining modular components, light-filled rooms, and open plans to create homes he described as "machines for living." In 1925, German architect Walter Gropius designed a new building for the Bauhaus school of art, architecture, and design that is generally considered the first example of what would become the international style of architecture. Stripped down to a steel frame and glass curtain wall, with no extraneous decoration, Gropius's Bauhaus stood in contrast to the art deco extravagance of the Chrysler Building.

With the rise of the Nazis, many modernist architects fled to the United States, where modernist architecture developed into the international style, which was characterized by the use of steel, reinforced concrete, large areas of glass, a uniform facade, and an absence of applied ornament. The international style became the

The Seagram Building, designed by Ludwig Mies van der Rohe and Philip Johnson, is a masterpiece of twentieth-century international style architecture.

dominant global architectural style after World War II. Critics initially praised the international style as a practical response to the needs of the masses. For several decades, this style provided uniformity for large-scale architectural projects. In the hands of master architects such as Le Corbusier and Ludwig Mies van der Rohe, modernist buildings were often elegant manifestations of Mies van der Rohe's famous dictum that "less is more"—subtly and austerely beautiful. In less inspired hands, such buildings were often unadorned, functional, and interchangeable glass blocks.

"LESS IS BORE"

Buildings that were considered **avant-garde** in 1930 became the norm by the mid-twentieth century. Architects who wanted to make a statement experimented with new materials and forms while retaining the concepts of clean lines and a lack of ornamentation. Buildings such as Frank Lloyd Wright's Guggenheim Museum (1959) and Bertrand Goldberg's Marina City (1964) abandoned the glass box in favor of sculptured curves.

In 1966, Philadelphia architect Robert Venturi declared war on the dominance of the international style in *Complexity and Contradiction in Architecture*. Proclaiming that "less is bore," Venturi challenged architects to create buildings that reflected their local and historical roots.

A variety of architectural movements sprang up in response. The postmodernists, championed by Michael Graves, Philip Johnson, and Venturi himself, returned to decoration and ornament, incorporating historical and vernacular elements into their designs, often with an ironic wink at the viewer. Neomodernists kept the core ideas of modernism but updated the way in which they were used. For example I. M. Pei's signature glass pyramids

I. M. Pei designed the Rock & Roll Hall of Fame, located in Cleveland, Ohio.

introduced new geometrical shapes, and Richard Meier's Getty Museum (1997) redefined the use of interior and exterior space. Deconstructivists took the idea "form follows fantasy" as their motto and created buildings with crooked walls, spiky angles, and fractured forms, meant to reflect the uncertainty of life at the end of the twentieth century. Advocates of high-tech style celebrated technology by making pipes and conduits principal elements of their designs—giving "form follows function" new meaning. The premier example of this style is the Centre Pompidou

(1977), in which the architectural firm Piano and Rogers placed the building's pipes, ductwork, electrical conduits, and elevators outside the glass curtain wall.

At the same time that architects were reinventing the skyscraper, a small handful of architects and engineers were reaching toward the sky in a very different way and experimenting with ways to use solar power to heat homes.

Heliotrope, designed by Rolf Disch, rotates so that its solar panels can track the sun.

CHAPTER 5
Solar Technology

Humans have always used the direct energy of the sun—to dry meat, fish, vegetables, and fruit to keep them from spoiling; to heat water; and to dry laundry.

Once humans invented glass, we soon found ways to intensify the effects of sunlight, creating solar heat traps and "burning mirrors" first with clear glass and later with actual mirrors. Builders in ancient Rome installed glass windows in the southern walls of public baths to warm them, and *heliocamus*, or "solar furnace," rooms were common enough in the homes of the wealthy that lawsuits over "sun rights" appear in court records.

The Romans also built the first small-scale greenhouses: glazed glass boxes that allowed the emperor Tiberius to indulge his taste for cucumbers all year long. By the mid-fifteenth century, Korean gardeners used greenhouses to grow out-of-season fruits and vegetables. In the sixteenth century, gardeners in Europe experimented with the same technology. Greenhouses came of age in the eighteenth century, when new glass-manufacturing methods allowed the production of large plates of glass. Functional greenhouses, designed to extend the growing season of native crops and allow the cultivation of delicacies from warmer climates, gave birth to conservatories: glassed-in ornamental gardens for the rich.

LOOKING for ALTERNATIVE ENERGY in the EIGHTEENTH and NINETEENTH CENTURIES

In the eighteenth century, natural philosophers (the name used by scientists at the time) asked new questions about the nature of energy. Using the scientific method of observation, measurement, and testing of hypotheses that had been developed over the past century, a few men experimented with the power of the sun. Those experiments resulted in several innovative scientific tools, the best known being Swiss naturalist Horace de Saussure's (1740–1799) hot box and French chemist Antoine Lavoisier's (1743–1794) solar furnace.

In 1767, Saussure built the first solar collector in an attempt to trap and measure solar heat. He constructed a miniature greenhouse from five glass boxes that fit inside each other like nested Russian dolls. Saussure covered the bottom of each box with a black coating that would absorb heat and exposed the apparatus to the sun for several hours, rotating it so that the sun's rays continuously struck it from the same angle. When he measured the temperature inside the boxes, he found had trapped enough thermal energy that he could use the innermost box as a thermal oven.

Lavoisier built the first solar furnace as part of his work in thermochemistry. The furnace focused the heat of the sun through large curved lenses filled with vinegar. He used the furnace as a heat source for experiments because he was concerned about contamination from the by-products of fuel combustion. It produced enough heat that Lavoisier could burn a diamond in air in an insulated jar.

With the advent of the Industrial Revolution at the end of the eighteenth century, the question of solar power took on new importance. The first factory machines were powered by water, but water was soon replaced by the steam engine. Steam engines needed coal or wood to run—using one form of power to produce another.

Some men believed that solar power could be harnessed to run steam engines. French mathematician Augustin Mouchot (1825–1911) and Swedish American engineer John Ericsson (1803–1889), best known for designing the Civil War ironclad *Monitor*, were among those who experimented with hot boxes, parabolic mirrors, and solar-driven pumps in their efforts to produce enough solar power to drive industrial steam engines.

Fred Keck's House of Tomorrow, a modernist house built for the 1933 Century of Progress, inspired his continued work on solar houses.

FRANK LLOYD WRIGHT'S SOLAR HEMICYCLE (1946–1948)

Frank Lloyd Wright's Solar Hemicycle, built in Madison, Wisconsin, for Herbert and Katherine Jacobs, explored the idea of a solar house in symbolic as well as functional terms.

Wright's design works much like Keck's solar houses as far as the technology is concerned. A large expanse of glass on the south wall captures the sun's heat, which is absorbed by a concrete floor and limestone walls on the first floor. The second floor is a balcony, suspended from the roof joists and pulled back from the glazed window to the south, allowing solar-heated air to rise into the second floor without obstruction. A radiant heat system imbedded in the floor provides supplementary heat to the solar-warmed floor. An overhanging roof on the south and bermed walls on the north, east, and west ensure that the house stays cool in summer.

But while most solar houses are linear in form, the Solar Hemicycle is a segment of a circle. Although it gives the impression of being a full semicircle, it is not. While the roofline stretches across a full 180 degrees, the floor plan is, in fact, limited to 120 degrees. The 14-foot- (4.3 m) tall arc of glass on the south wall spans the two stories of the house for only 90 degrees. This glass wall faces onto a circular sunken garden, which echoes the house's circular form. As the sun moves across the sky, it tracks the floor plan—turning the idea of a solar house into a metaphor as well as a heating system.

Frank Lloyd Wright's Solar Hemicycle turned passive solar heating into art.

The FIRST SOLAR HOUSES

In the eighteenth and nineteen centuries, experiments with solar power focused on scientific and industrial applications. In the twentieth century, architects and engineers looked for ways to use solar energy to heat houses.

There are two ways to heat a house with solar energy. Passive solar systems take in sunlight through windows and store it in some form of thermal mass, commonly concrete, brick, stone, or tile. Active solar heating uses mechanical heat traps and storage systems, often built on principles similar to those Saussure used in his hot box.

The first attempts to design houses heated by solar energy occurred in the 1930s and 1940s, driven by the scarcities of the Great Depression and the energy shortages of the Second World War. Architects and engineers looked for inexpensive and reliable ways to heat homes that did not rely on nonrenewable fossil fuels.

Illinois architectural engineer Fred Keck (1895–1980) was the first American architect to apply principles of solar heating to houses. He initially became interested in the concept of heating houses with passive solar energy as the result of the House of Tomorrow, a modernist glass house he designed for the 1933 Century of Progress in Chicago. The twelve-sided building was effectively a greenhouse. It was swelteringly hot in the summer, but any solar warmth it took in during the winter immediately dissipated through its single-glazed glass walls.

Keck built a series of solar houses throughout the 1930s. With each house he learned new lessons about building orientation, glass placement, and the use of shade. He learned to orient the house to the southern exposure. He experimented with building a house's northern exposure into an earth berm and using evaporation pools on the roof to help cool the house in the summer. He borrowed an idea from the Japanese and installed supplemental heat in the floors. He created exterior Venetian blinds and built roof overhangs to control the amount of sun that entered the house, borrowing the latter idea from Frank Lloyd Wright's Robie House. He installed ventilating louvers under windows to let in fresh air—a device previously used only in garages and attics. He used double-glazed insulated glass, which was first introduced in 1935 and proved to be a critical element in building efficient passive solar houses.

Keck quickly discovered that heating a solar house is the easy part. The hard part is keeping the house cool. Houses had to be designed to keep the sun out when it was not wanted. Keck went to the Adler Planetarium for help in determining the angles at which the sun struck the Chicago area over the course of the year. He used the information to develop architectural shading diagrams, which showed the angles at which the sun would hit a building's window at various points during the day. Such diagrams are now standard design tools for architects.

Keck built his first successful solar house in 1940 for real estate developer Howard Sloan in Glenview, Illinois. It was the first building to be described using the term "solar house." The Sloan House includes all the major design elements used in building passive solar houses today. Keck elongated the floor plan so all the major rooms faced south. Double-glazed plate glass windows filled most of the south wall, which was shaded by a roof overhang that tilted upward, limiting the amount of summer sun that reached the windows while letting in the winter sun, which is lower to the horizon. As a result, the house took advantage of solar heat in the winter while remaining cool in the summer. Encouraged by his success, Keck and Sloan went

These experimental solar houses were built in the 1970s and designed to use active solar technology.

on to develop a twenty-four unit solar-heated subdivision in Glenview, called Solar Park.

By 1942, Keck had defined the essential elements of a passive solar house. He worked closely with glass manufacturer Libby-Owens-Ford to educate the public about the benefits of solar houses and architects about the technical issues involved in designing them.

ACTIVE SOLAR HOUSES

At the same time Keck and others were designing passive solar houses, a team of MIT engineers, led by chemical engineer Hoyt C. Hottel, was exploring whether active solar heating was feasible.

In 1939, Hottel's team built the first of three solar houses that used rooftop solar collectors and water storage tanks to capture and store solar energy. They did not describe the building we now know as MIT Solar House I as a "solar house" at the time. In fact, it was not an actual house. Only 558 square feet (51.8 sq m) in size, it consisted of an office and an instrument room built over a 17,000-gallon (64,352-liter) water storage tank. The team installed fourteen flat-plate solar collectors on the sloped roof.

Flat-plate collectors, sometimes called "Hottel collectors," are descendants of Saussure's hot box. In their most basic form, they are black-lined boxes with glass tops. The sun shines through the glass top and is absorbed by the dark-colored absorber plates. As heat builds up in the collector, it is transferred to pipes carrying water. The hot water is collected in a storage tank, from which it is distributed through the building's heating system.

Hottel's team had two goals: to test the relative efficiency of different types of flat-plate collectors and to test whether heat could be stored in a water tank in the summer and used to heat the building in the winter. The technology successfully maintained the building's interior at 72 degrees Fahrenheit (22 degrees Celsius) for three winters without any supplemental heat. Hottel's combination of solar collectors and storage tank remained the fundamental design that would power thousands of solar homes built in the 1970s and 1980s.

Engineers and architects continued to experiment with solar architecture throughout the 1950s, but as the general economic climate in the United States swung from scarcity to abundance, people became less interested in conserving energy. Traditional features designed to make homes more comfortable in warm weather, such as breezeways, screened sleeping porches, and awnings, disappeared in favor of tightly sealed windows and air conditioning.

In the 1960s, the impetus for solar design came from environmental activists. Designers like rocket engineer and environmentalist Peter van Dresser found creative and low-tech solutions to the challenges of solar heating. Often combining solar heating with other environmentally friendly technologies, such as wind power, they designed unconventional houses using both indigenous traditions, like adobe, and reclaimed industrial materials, such as salvaged auto parts. They built them in shapes inspired by crystals and geodesic domes.

Despite the creativity with which environmental activists transformed the art and science of solar housing, it took the 1973 OPEC oil embargo to bring solar houses back into the political and scientific mainstream. With the introduction of a federal tax credit for residential solar heating systems in 1978, major corporations began manufacturing solar collectors for home use. By 1984, more than one million American homes adopted some form of solar technology.

The OTHER SOLAR TECHNOLOGY

Converting solar energy to electricity requires different technology than using solar energy to heat a house.

The basic unit for converting sunlight into electricity is the solar cell, also called a photovoltaic (PV) cell. Solar cells are typically made from two thin layers of silicon that have been treated to form an electric field, with one positive charge and one negative. When sunlight hits a solar cell, the silicon atoms absorb some of the light. The light's energy knocks electrons out of the silicon, which then flow between the two layers, creating an electric current that can be captured and used.

A single solar cell does not produce enough electricity to run anything, so solar cells are grouped together into solar panels. To provide even more electricity, several panels can be connected together to form a solar array.

Solar cell technology began in 1839, when French physicist Edmond Becquerel (1820–1891) discovered that exposing certain substances to light created an electric current in metals and liquids, a principal known as the **photovoltaic effect**. Four decades later, American inventor Charles Fritts created the first solar cells from thin wafers of selenium, an element derived from copper ore. He hoped his solar cells would compete with Thomas Edison's coal-fired power plants, which opened the year before, but his cells converted only 1 percent of the sunlight that hit their surface into electric power—not enough for practical use.

The real breakthroughs in producing usable solar cells came at Bell Laboratories in the mid-twentieth century. In 1940, semiconductor researcher Russell Ohls created what he described as a "light-sensitive electric device" from a cracked silicon sample. Ohls's device was still only 1 percent efficient, but it provided a theoretical foundation for the team that created the first practical solar cells in 1954—engineer Daryl Chapin, chemist Calvin Fuller, and physicist Gerald Pearson. When the team first demonstrated solar cells in operation on April 25, 1954, the media responded with articles predicting solar-powered fans, lawnmowers, and a solar-powered convertible that would steer itself while passengers sat in the back. A few even suggested that solar power could provide the world with cheap, clean energy.

The first solar cells were too expensive for commercial use, but the United States military funded additional research aimed at using PV technology to power satellites. The United States Naval Research Laboratory launched the first solar-powered satellite, Vanguard I, in 1958. Solar cells still power satellites and other space equipment today.

As the cost of solar panels goes down, more and more architects incorporate them into building designs. Heliotrope (1994), created by German architect Rolf Disch, is a particularly dramatic example. One of the first homes in the world to produce more energy than it uses, the entire house rotates to track the sun. Other uses of photovoltaic technology in buildings are barely noticeable: PV roof shingles and coatings for windows allow any house to produce its own electricity.

Today, solar panels power road signs, radio transmitters, and parking meters, as well as satellites and space vehicles. They even power runway lights on airstrips in Antarctica. Because they do not need to be attached to power lines, they can also power houses that are not connected to the power grid, in places as different as the Himalayan Mountains and the Australian bush.

The use of solar energy in buildings is part of a larger architectural concern with creating sustainable, environmentally friendly buildings—a concern that is one of the driving forces in architecture today.

Frank Gehry's Guggenheim Museum in Bilbao, Spain, was designed using software developed for the aerospace industry.

CHAPTER 6
Architecture Today and Tomorrow

The defining image of ancient Egypt is the pyramid. For medieval Europe, it's the Gothic cathedral. The skyscraper in all its variations was the definitive building style of the twentieth century. We don't know yet what the defining architectural model of the twenty-first century will be. New technologies and new twists on old technology make new types of buildings possible. Social concerns, such as environmental issues and crowded cities, shape architectural choices in new ways. Architects are designing both buildings in which every piece is custom made and buildings that are made entirely of prefabricated modular parts. All these design trends are based in the core belief that the architect's job is not simply to design buildings but to design a better world.

SUSTAINABLE ARCHITECTURE: REDUCE, REUSE, RECYCLE

Architects and their clients are increasingly concerned with creating environmentally friendly buildings.

One popular goal for new buildings is net zero energy: creating an energy-efficient building that produces at least as much energy as it uses in a year. In order to design a net zero energy building, an architect must consider all the ways in which a building's occupants consume energy, not just heating and cooling. The final design needs to reduce the amount of energy the building uses and create systems that generate and recover energy, often using both passive and active solar technologies.

Reducing energy use is the most obvious issue that architects attack when designing green buildings, but alternative energy sources and passive solar technologies are not the only ways in which architects can achieve environmental goals. Using more sustainable materials, using less material, and recycling previously used materials all help reduce the environmental impact of building construction. Considering a material's ability to retain or dispel heat can improve a building's energy use. Materials with recycled content not only use less new material but often require less energy and chemicals to produce. Sustainably harvested and rapidly renewable materials, such as bamboo or products made from agricultural waste, do less damage to the ecosystem. Utilizing local materials avoids the ecological impact of transportation and supports local economies. More vigorous approaches to sustainable architecture also look at reducing water consumption, reusing wastewater, and reducing the creation of waste.

The initial cost of building sustainable architecture is often higher than standard construction. In order to create green buildings, architects must make hard choices, balancing questions of resource use, cost, and human comfort.

Designing for Deconstruction

Instead of building for eternity, like the pharaohs of Egypt, some architects design buildings that are easy to take apart when they are no longer useful, built with materials that can be reused or recycled. The underlying idea is that most structures have a limited useful life in an ever-changing society, whether it's four years or one hundred. Instead of allowing a building to decay or adapting it to new use, they argue that it is more ecologically sound to disassemble it.

It's not an entirely new idea. The Crystal Palace, for instance, was designed so that it could be disassembled and moved when the exhibition came to an end. The same idea is already used in designing housing for disaster relief and temporary military buildings. One example of this type of design is David Miller's prizewinning Pavilion in the Park (2007), an 11,100 square-foot (1,031.2 sq m) open-plan exhibition center in Seattle. Miller designed the building so it could be broken down into four modules, each of which can be disassembled and relocated. The modular plan also means that the building can be expanded or reduced in size as needed.

From an environmental standpoint, designs of this type allow more of the material to be reused than when an existing building is demolished. In part, that is because architects make design choices that make it easier to separate different materials from each other—using screws instead of nails or glue, for instance—or that use larger units of construction material, which are more likely to be reused.

Biomimicry

Some of the most exciting experiments in sustainable architecture are based on the principle of biomimicry, the practice of finding solutions in nature and applying them to human designs.

Biomimicry has a long history. Brunelleschi, for instance, is reported to have found his solution for building a strong, light dome for the cathedral in Florence by studying eggshells. In the eighteenth century, French scientist René Réaumur's study of wasp nests led papermakers to use wood pulp rather than cotton and linen

One Central Park's hydroponic gardens create living "green walls," adding shade and filtering out direct sun.

rags. Swiss engineer George de Mestral invented Velcro after he noticed how cockleburs stuck to his wool pants and in his dog's fur.

Modern architects look to natural structures hoping to find better solutions for problems such as temperature control, carbon emissions, and zero-waste systems. For instance, the way skin pores open and close inspired Tobias Becker of the University of Stuttgart to develop pneumatic architectural facades that control the flow of air and light into a building by adjusting their permeability.

One of the most successful examples of biomimicry in building design is the Eastgate Centre (1996) in Harare, Zimbabwe. The building uses passive energy strategies inspired by Africa's gigantic termite mounds, which use the earth's moisture and thermal mass, internal ventilation shafts, and changes in external temperature over the course of the day to maintain a constant internal temperature. Mud chambers inside a termite mound capture heat during the day and release it at night. Ventilation shafts draw in cool air from intake holes low in the mound and expel it from the top using stack ventilation—the same principle that pulls smoke up a chimney. The Eastgate Centre's passive ventilation system mimics both techniques, keeping its occupants comfortable with little need for mechanical heating or air conditioning.

Green Walls

Some architects are incorporating living plants into buildings to add shade and filter out sunlight, making structures that are literally green.

Green walls, sometimes called living walls, are vertical gardens that are attached directly to a building's structure. In a true vertical garden, the plants are grown hydroponically, which means they are fed mineral nutrients in water instead of growing in soil. Water and nutrients are supplied to the gardens through the structure of the building itself. Because no soil is used, the plants do not threaten the building's structural integrity. This architectural technique is most popular in hot climates. Zimbabwe's Eastgate Centre, for instance, combines green walls on two sides of the building with jagged edges on its facade to create shade where none would otherwise exist. Similarly, One Central Park (2013), a 33-story mixed-use building in Sydney, Australia, is covered in a living skin of 180,000 plants—some 350 different varieties of plants in 23 separate vertical gardens as well as terraced gardens.

Green walls can also be incorporated on a smaller scale, as Vo Trong Nghia Architects demonstrated with Stacking Green, a prizewinning single-family house in Ho Chi Minh City. The house is long and narrow, a style known as a "tube house" that is common in Vietnamese cities. Twelve concrete planters, spaced according to the height of the plants, cover two facades of the house, allowing natural light to filter into the house without increasing its internal temperature. In a city that experiences high heat, heavy rains, and daylong power outages, this design keeps the house cool and well lit with little energy use.

BUILDING BLOCKS

Affordable housing is a critical issue in many parts of the world. Developing countries suffer serious housing crises caused by growing populations and migration to cities. Natural and political disasters leave many homeless and stranded in shantytowns and refugee camps. Cities in the United States and Western Europe suffer from a lack of well-built affordable housing for those at the bottom of the economic ladder. Architects are increasingly exploring modular construction as a way to build attractive housing that is affordable and easily constructed.

Tokyo architect Shigeru Ban was one of the earliest to experiment with ways to build high-quality, low-cost shelters for disaster victims, making clever use of materials such as cardboard and shipping containers. He built his first structures using cardboard tubes as a series of case studies in 1985 and 1986. Cardboard houses became more than a theoretical exercise in 1994, when Ban learned about the horrible housing conditions in camps created by the United Nations to house two million refugees from the Rwandan Civil War. He created a prototype for emergency shelters made of a framework of paper tubes covered with the plastic blankets provided by the UN.

Ban went on to found the Voluntary Architects' Network (VAN), through which he has built temporary housing for disaster victims around the world. He designed a prototype for permanent houses made from local timber and compressed earth blocks to replace a Sri Lankan fishing village that was swept away in the

2004 tsunami. Built with local labor as well as local materials, the one-story houses were designed to accommodate the physical needs of a tropical climate and the social needs of a traditional Muslim community. He designed temporary homes from stacked shipping containers for Japanese disaster victims after the 2011 tsunami and was involved in the Make It Right housing project in New Orleans following Hurricane Katrina. Not satisfied with building emergency housing, Ban also created a temporary church and community center in Kobe, Japan, after the 1995 earthquake, as well as a cathedral built from cardboard tubes and colored-glass triangles in Christchurch, New Zealand, to replace the Anglican cathedral destroyed in the earthquake that struck the city in 2011.

An innovative design for temporary housing for victims of the 2011 Onagawa tsunami made from stacked shipping containers

More recently, Ban designed modular housing for those made homeless by the earthquakes in Nepal in 2015. Intended to be permanent structures rather than emergency relief, these houses are made with wood frames that can be filled in with rubble taken from the piles of debris created by the earthquakes. The roof is made with thatch, built over a truss system of cardboard tubes. People can move in as soon as the frame and roof are complete, adding the rubble filler after they have a basic shelter.

Housing shortages also create a need for flexible, affordable buildings. Mexico, for instance, with one of the fastest growing populations in Latin America, needs an estimated nine million new homes. Architect Tatiana Bilbao responded to that need with a design for a pitched-roof house that can be adapted to meet the needs of different families. The house is built around a rigid core of concrete blocks. The surrounding modules are made of more lightweight materials, such as recycled wooden pallets. Additional modules can be added as a family grows or to accommodate the addition of a small business. The design can be adapted for different cultures or terrains, using locally available materials.

Vietnam-based Vo Trong Nghia Architects have also addressed the question of how to solve housing shortages, creating a design that can be mass-produced and easily shipped to wherever it is needed. Their S-house was designed with Vietnam's Mekong Delta in mind. Built with a galvanized steel structure and a concrete foundation, the house is strong and flexible enough to withstand earthquakes and other natural disasters. Each component weighs less than 130 pounds (59 kilograms) and can fit in a standard shipping container for easy transport. The frame can be assembled in less than three hours. The architects sheathed the prototype with palm leaves, but the house could be finished with any locally available material or industrial building product. The firm hopes to extend the S-house project to other parts of the world where low-income people suffer from inadequate housing. An S-house can be built for as little as $1,000.

Each of these projects, and others like them, whether designed for homeless refuges in Rwanda or homeless teens in London, are part of a broader trend of socially minded architecture.

NEW SHAPES

At the other end of the architectural spectrum from using modular units to create affordable housing are dramatic public buildings that can best be described as sculptural. Some are almost fractal in their appearance, as if the architect was an origami artist who took the glass box of the international style and folded it into another shape altogether. Other buildings do away with hard edges, featuring curving forms and folds that seem at once organic and fantastical. Both approaches are made possible with the use of 3D design software, which allows architects to experiment with complex shapes and engineers to make structural calculations that would not have been possible fifteen years ago.

The most famous practitioner of sculptural architecture is Frank Gehry (b. 1929). His design for the Guggenheim Museum in Bilbao, Spain, is the definitive building in this style. Designed to resemble a giant ship, an allusion to Bilbao's history as an important port, the building's complex forms, constructed of titanium tiles, limestone, and glass, curve and twist until the metaphorical form of the ship is nearly lost. Using software developed for the aerospace industry rather than what was then standard CAD software, his aim was to create a form that the viewer can't hold in her mind, one that changes depending on the angle from which it is seen.

Instead of internal steel frames providing a skeleton for sculptural buildings, many are supported primarily by their exterior surface—a practice described as a "**structural skin**."

ALEJANDRO ARAVENA'S INCREMENTAL HOUSING

Chilean architect Alejandro Aravena, winner of the 2016 Pritzker Architecture Prize, says architects shouldn't think of themselves as artists. Instead, their primary goal should be to use their designs to improve the way people live.

In 2001, in conjunction with engineer Andres Iacobelli, Aravena founded Elemental, which bills itself as a "do tank," as opposed to a "think tank." Elemental concentrates on what Aravena describes as "projects of public interest and social impact." They work with communities that are poor or recovering from disasters to identify key social needs and individual desires as part of the design process—what Aravena calls "participatory design."

His best-known innovation is incremental housing, sometimes known as "Half a House." Working from the philosophy that government-supported affordable housing should focus on what families cannot provide for themselves, the "Half a House" model gives each family a two-story house, only 431 square feet (40 sq m), with a kitchen, bathroom, and two small rooms, and an empty plot of land of the same size next to it. Families build out the other half of the house to suit their own needs when they can afford it, creating

As curator of the 2016 Venice Architectural Biennial, Alejandro Aravena sought to expand the issues to which architects respond.

individualized houses from a uniform design. Aravena first implemented this type of incremental architecture at the Quinta Monroy housing project in Iquique, Chile, in 2003.

When Aravena received the Pritzker Prize, he announced he had published plans for four of his social housing projects on his website, making them available for anyone to use.

One of the most explicit examples of this concept is the Beijing National Stadium, built for the 2008 Olympic Games by the Swiss architectural firm Herzog & De Meuron in collaboration with Chinese artist Ai Weiwei. Nicknamed the "Bird's Nest," the stadium is an elliptical bowl made up of a structural framework of interwoven diagonal steel beams that curve up to encase the central concrete core of the stands.

NEW MATERIALS CREATE NEW POSSIBILITIES

New building materials could change the way we build in the future. Some new materials are designed to solve old problems in innovative ways. Self-healing concrete, for instance, combines concrete mix with bacteria and calcium lactate capsules. When cracks form in the concrete, water activates the bacteria, which eat the capsules. The bacteria then produce calcite, which fills in the cracks. Meanwhile, pollutant-absorbing pavement uses energy from the sun to break down polluted air into water and oxygen, cleaning both the pavement and the air around it.

Other new materials change the essential nature of familiar materials, thereby opening new possibilities, just as new ways of making steel made skyscrapers possible. Researchers at Sweden's KTH Royal Institute of Technology, for instance, developed a transparent wood composite that combines the translucence of glass with the strength of traditional lumber. It could be used to build transparent wooden structures, create load-bearing windows that would never break, or develop new types of solar panels made from wood instead of glass.

Several companies are experimenting with growing building materials from bacteria. Agricultural waste has been combined with mushroom mycelium to create bricks that can be grown in molds in five days. These bricks are lightweight and have a higher compression strength than concrete. Peter Trimble, a design student at University of Edinburgh, created a concrete alternative using sand and *Sporosarcina pasteurii*, a bacterium that is sometimes used to solidify soil to hold posts in place. Both products require less energy to produce and are more sustainable than their traditional counterparts. Who knows what the combination of lighter weight and great strength will make possible?

Architecture is once again poised at the crossroads of art and technology. New technologies, like 3D printers that can shape glass into new forms or elevators that can move without vertical cables, offer architects the capacity to build in ways we have never built before. Who knows what we will build next?

GLOSSARY

arch A curved structure spanning an opening. It is built of carefully fitted stones or other material and is capable of supporting its own weight and the weight of any structure above it.

avant-garde Innovative ideas that push the boundaries of the accepted norm, generally used in reference to culture and the arts.

basilica In the Roman Empire, a long public hall with a wide central aisle. In early Christian architecture, this form was adapted for use as a church.

bitumen A naturally occurring asphalt-like substance that seeps to Earth's surface in Iraq. Bitumen was often used as cement and mortar in the ancient Middle East.

buttress A projecting structure that supports a load-bearing wall.

coffering Recessed panels in a ceiling. They are used both as decoration and to lighten the weight in a vault or dome.

compressive strength The ability to support a load (compression stress) without being crushed or buckling. Also known as compression strength.

curtain wall An exterior wall with no load-bearing function. Curtain walls can be made of any material, but the term often refers to the exterior glass walls of skyscrapers.

dome A rounded vault, which usually covers a circular or square space.

dressed stone Stone which has been cut to a specific shape and given a smooth finish on at least one side.

fieldstone Literally the rocks removed from a field in preparation for farming. Fieldstone is used as a building material without shaping or finishing.

flying buttress Half-arches applied to the exterior of a building to counteract the lateral thrust of the interior rib vaults. Flying buttresses are one of the defining features of Gothic architecture.

hypostyle hall A large room in which the roof is supported by interior pillars.

keystone The central stone of an arch, which locks the wedge-shaped stones of the arch in place.

megalith Literally an enormous stone. "Megalith" is generally used to refer to the stone constructions of Bronze Age Europe.

photovoltaic effect The creation of an electrical current when certain substances are exposed to sunlight.

post-and-lintel A construction technique in which two upright architectural members (the posts) support a horizontal third (the lintel). This technique is also known as a trabeated structure.

structural skin The use of a building's exterior surface as its primary structural support, a term borrowed from the aeronautics industry.

tensile strength The ability to resist forces that stretch a structural element.

vault An extended or continuous arch, usually covering a rectangular space.

vernacular architecture Architecture built by local craftsmen using local materials in a traditional style, often without the help of an architect.

ziggurat A stepped pyramid.

FURTHER INFORMATION

BOOKS

Denzer, Anthony. *The Solar House: Pioneering Sustainable Design*. New York: Rizzoli International Publishing, 2013.

Strickland, Carol. *The Annotated Arch: A Crash Course in the History of Architecture*. Kansas City, MO: Andrews McMeel Publishing, 2001.

WEBSITES

ArchDaily
http://www.archdaily.com
This website is a great source for the latest architectural news.

Chicago Architecture Foundation Visual Dictionary
http://www.architecture.org/architecture-chicago/visual-dictionary
Photographs and information about buildings, architects, and architectural concepts.

VIDEOS

Building Big

http://www.pbs.org/wgbh/buildingbig

Building Big is five-part PBS series hosted by author David Macaulay about building bridges, domes, skyscrapers, dams, and tunnels.

How Buildings Learn

https://www.youtube.com/watch?v=AvEqfg2sIH0

This six-part, three-hour BBC series, based on Stewart Brand's book of the same title, offers a critique of modern architecture and argues in favor of smaller scale, organically designed buildings.

ORGANIZATIONS and MUSEUMS

Chicago Architectural Foundation

http://www.architecture.org

The Chicago Architectural Foundation (CAF) has a wide-ranging mission that includes educational programs, tours, and conservation efforts.

Pritzker Architecture Prize

http://www.pritzkerprize.com

One of the preeminent prizes in the field, the Pritzker Architecture Prize was established in 1979. The organization's website includes information about how prizewinners are selected, the history of the award, and biographies of laureates.

Skyscraper Museum

http://www.skyscraper.org

The Skyscraper Museum is located in New York City and hosts are range of permanent and rotating exhibitions. The museum's website is a great resource for students; it includes an extensive archive of lectures and digital collections.

BIBLIOGRAPHY

Arnold, Dieter. *Building in Egypt: Pharonic Stone Masonry*. Oxford, UK: Oxford University Press, 1991.

Bartlett, John R. *Jericho*. Cambridge, UK: Lutteworth Press,1982.

Bertman, Stephen. *Handbook to Life in Ancient Mesopotamia*. New York: Facts on File, 2003.

Butti, Ken and John Perlin. *A Golden Thread: 2500 Years of Solar Architecture and Technology*. Palo Alto, CA: Chesire Books, 1980.

Clarke, Sommers and R. Engelbach. *Ancient Egyptian Construction and Architecture*. New York: Dover Publications, 1980.

Denzer, Anthony. *The Solar House: Pioneering Sustainable Design.* New York: Rizzoli, 2013.

Huxtable, Ada Louise. *The Tall Building Artistically Reconsidered: The Search for a Skyscraper Style*. New York: Pantheon Books, 1982

King, Ross. *Brunelleschi's Dome: How a Renaissance Genius Reinvented Architecture*. New York: Bloomsbury, 2000.

Klanton, Robertt, Sven Ehmann, and Sofia Borges, eds. *The Sky's the Limit: Applying Radical Architecture*. Berlin: Gestaltan, 2012.

Macaulay, David. *Pyramid*. Boston: Houghton Mifflin Company, 1975.

———. *Cathedral: The Story of Its Construction*. Boston: Houghton Mifflin Company, 1973.

Maclay, William. *The New Net Zero: Leading-Edge Design and Construction of Homes and Buildings for a Renewable Energy Future*. White River Junction, VT: Chelsea Green Publishing, 2014.

Mitchell, George. *The Hindu Temple: An Introduction to Its Meaning and Forms*. New York: Harper and Row, 1977.

Stout, Geraldine, and Matthew Stout. *Newgrange*. Cork, Ireland: Cork University Press, 2008.

Thorpe, Martin. *Roman Architecture*. London: Bristol Classical Press, 1995.

Van Beek, Gus W., and Ora Van Beek. *Glorious Mud! Ancient and Contemporary Earthen Design and Construction in North Africa, Western Europe, the Near East, and Southwest Asia.* Washington, DC: Smithsonian Institution in conjunction with Rowman and Littlefield Publsihers, 2008.

Watson, Sally. *Building the New Millennium: Architecture at the Start of the 21st Century*. London: Phaidon, 2009.

Wickham-Jones, Caroline. *Between the Wind and the Water: World Heritage Orkney*. Macclesfield, UK: Windgather Press, 2006.

Wright, G. R. H. *Ancient Building Technology*. Leiden, Holland: Brill, 2000.

INDEX

Page numbers in **boldface** are illustrations. Entries in **boldface** are glossary terms.

ABOUT the AUTHOR

Pamela D. Toler is a freelance writer with a PhD in history and a lifelong fascination with buildings. Her work has appeared in *Aramco World, Calliope, History Channel Magazine, MHQ: The Quarterly Journal of Military History*, and *Victorian Home*. She is the author of a biography of Matt Damon; *The Everything Guide to Understanding Socialism; Mankind: The Story of All of Us*, companion volume to the History Channel series of the same name; and, most recently, *Heroines of Mercy Street: The Real Nurses of the Civil War*, a nonfiction companion to the PBS historical drama *Mercy Street*. She currently lives in Chicago, the home of the skyscraper. You can find her at her website, www.pameladtoler.com.